CW00407408

[illegible]

Printed in Great Britain
by Amazon

71755011R00058